EXPECTING

Christmas

EXPECTING

Christmas

Daily Readings *for the* Season of Joy

NEW HOPE®
PUBLISHERS
Imprint of Iron Stream Media
BIRMINGHAM, ALABAMA

New Hope® Publishers
100 Missionary Ridge
Birmingham, AL 35242
NewHopePublishers.com
An imprint of Iron Stream Media
IronStreamMedia.com

© 2015, 2016 by Iron Stream Media, compiled by the staff
of Iron Stream Media
All rights reserved. First printing 2019.
Printed in the United States of America.

Library of Congress Cataloging-in-Publication Data

Title: Expecting Christmas : daily readings for the season of joy.
Description: First [edition]. | Birmingham : New Hope Publishers,
    an imprint of Iron Stream Media, 2019.
Identifiers: LCCN 2019000475 | ISBN 9781563092541 (permabind)
Subjects: LCSH: Christmas—Meditations. | Advent—Meditations.
Classification: LCC BV45 .E97 2019 | DDC 242/.33—dc23
LC record available at https://lccn.loc.gov/2019000475

ISBN-13: 978-1-56309-254-1
Ebook ISBN: 978-1-56309-165-0

1 2 3 4 5—22 21 20 19 18

Contents

EXPECTING

Christmas

Day 1

Therefore the L<small>ORD</small> himself will give you a sign. Behold, the virgin shall conceive and bear a son, and shall call his name Immanuel. —Isaiah 7:14

If you have spent any amount of time on the Internet, you've probably seen videos of soldiers returning home from overseas as they reunite with loved ones. Whether the videos are of a soldier surprising a spouse, a child, or even a dog, they have captured people's hearts and garnered millions of views. Why is that? For one thing, people can relate to that powerful sense of relief and joy upon reuniting with a loved one. We can put ourselves in the place of these men, women, children, and, yes, even dogs. We vicariously enjoy their excitement as they are reunited with loved ones.

Read Isaiah 7:10–14. Of all the messianic prophecies, verse 14 contains perhaps one of the most well known among believers today. This prophecy, like many messianic prophecies, had what Christian commentators call a "near" and "far" fulfillment. The near fulfillment specifically related to King Ahaz and Jerusalem. The far fulfillment, however, has one clear, inarguable meaning—the miraculous birth of Christ by a virgin. Truly, Jesus was *and* is Immanuel, "God with us," because of all the people born to a woman, He alone was *and* is God.

Can you imagine the sense of anticipation the people of God experienced as they meditated on the words of Isaiah 7:14? So many lived and died before the promise of this prophecy ever came to fruition. Advent is our time to pause and share in the experience of eagerly awaiting the Messiah. We remember Christ's birth, His death, and His Resurrection. And we also anticipate. As we fondly remember the ministry and salvation of Christ, we eagerly anticipate and await Christ's return.

Reflection

How might your life change if you were to spend more time anticipating the return of Christ?

What area(s) of your life do you experience the most struggle? In what ways might remembering Christ's ministry strengthen you in moments of difficulty or weakness?

God made a promise to send His Son, and He fulfilled that promise. Who in your life needs to be introduced to the trustworthiness of God, specifically as it relates to the promised Messiah?

Day 2

And the Word became flesh and dwelt among us, and we have seen his glory, glory as of the only Son from the Father, full of grace and truth. —John 1:14

Perhaps this has happened to you: you're sitting in a movie theater watching a trailer for an unreleased film and, after the short preview ends, you're suddenly so excited about the advertised movie that you've completely forgotten which movie you're about to watch. If done right, movie trailers will have you lined up at the ticket window on opening day. Like other types of advertisement, movie trailers are intended to be a film's representative to the world and are released to the public to show what the movie is about, what it stands for, and what kind of story it hopes to tell.

Read John 1:14–16. The Greek word for *word* in verse 14 is *logos*, which refers to the moral precepts and utterances of God. John stated that the Word, the utterances and teachings of God, became flesh. Jesus Christ was and is the physical representation of all God's decrees—all of God's grace and truth. More than that, the text also indicates that God Himself became human—He came as the God-man Jesus. John clarified that Jesus was more than an ambassador of the Word, more than a messenger of the Father, and more than a prophet of what was to come. Jesus is the Word made flesh—the only God the Son.

Not unlike a movie trailer, the teachings God gave His people throughout the Old Testament pointed to the coming of Christ and His future work in the world. Jesus was sent to the world to reveal to us the kind of story God wants to tell: a story of *grace upon grace*. The long-awaited Savior arrived, and people personally saw the glory of the Word made flesh with their own eyes. What an unspeakable blessing . . . to personally witness and study the glory of the Lord . . . especially when so many Old Testament believers had long anticipated the arrival of the Messiah.

Reflection

Jesus represented all the moral precepts of God. What teaching or verse in the Word is the most challenging to you? Why do you think that is?

Why do you think some people are more apt to eagerly anticipate the release of a movie than to eagerly await the return of Christ?

What are some ways you can prepare yourself to concisely present the story of Christ—think of it like a trailer—in order to stir anticipation in people's hearts for His return?

Day 3

*Glory to God in the highest, and on earth
peace among those with whom
He is pleased!* —Luke 2:14

In its simplest form, a story consists of a conflict, a climax, and a resolution. The conflict is the moment when all the rising tension in the story comes to a head and creates a problem that must be addressed. The climax is the moment when the rising tension following the conflict is finally confronted. And lastly, there's resolution, when all the rising tensions have rolled to a stop and the characters have their rest. And somewhere between the conflict and climax is something called the inciting incident that compels the main character to take action.

Read Luke 2:13–15. The gospel has always been in the mind of God, and the opening scene of the gospel story on earth is the birth of Christ. On this landmark night, the earth continued spinning and people continued going about their business. The night was quiet in the still town of Bethlehem. The locals slept. The world was oblivious to the history-changing event that had just taken place. Although earth was ignorant, heaven was aware. And heaven rejoiced!

Jesus left the right hand of the Father in heaven to be born to a virgin. Angels announced His birth not to the city leaders but to shepherds gathered in a field. It's as though the curtain were pulled back for a moment, and these shepherds were given a glimpse of the joyous celebration taking place in heaven. And then, just as suddenly, the curtain was drawn, and the night once again fell silent as though nothing had happened. But something had happened, and the world would never be the same.

The appearance of the angel to the shepherds was their inciting incident, the event that drove them to action and inevitably changed the course of their lives. The shepherds determine to act and go *straight* to Bethlehem. There was no time for deliberation. When the Lord makes Himself and His will so unquestionably clear to you, you obey.

Reflection

What have been a few inciting incidents in your life, moments that made you take action?

In what ways have you seen God at work in these moments?

Thank God for the moments that have shaped your life for the better. Pray that He will give you the boldness to act as obediently and decisively as the shepherds.

Day 4

Great indeed, we confess, is the mystery of godliness: He was manifested in the flesh, vindicated by the Spirit, seen by angels, proclaimed among the nations, believed on in the world, taken up in glory. —1 Timothy 3:16

*H*ave you ever heard of the term "elevator pitch"? This concept has become especially popular in business circles and is based on a simple idea: know your product or service well enough and concisely enough so you could give a detailed summary to someone during the length of time it would take to ride an elevator. Think about a hobby you are familiar with, such as sports, comics, or painting. Now, imagine that while you are on an elevator with someone, you have only until that person reaches his or her floor to summarize that hobby. Could you do it?

Read 1 Timothy 3:16. God was revealed in the flesh as the incarnation of Jesus Christ. The Word became flesh. The Messiah arrived. God the Son became a man. He was vindicated in the Spirit when the Spirit descended on Him as a sign to those present that He was who He claimed to be—the Messiah, God incarnate, who was completely righteous in the Father's eyes. Jesus' ministry captured the attention of those on earth and in heaven, both humans and angels alike. After His work was finished, Jesus ascended in glory and returned to the right hand of the Father. Not even Jesus' death could stop the forward motion of the gospel. His message and His name have continued to spread far and wide, bringing people of every nation to faith.

We were not called to be salespeople for the gospel, but we *are* called to make disciples. Therefore, it is necessary to know how to concisely present the story of Christ. Notice that 1 Timothy 3:16 is the perfect "elevator pitch" because it touches on the key points of the life of Christ. It is the message of the gospel in a nutshell. If you have difficulty knowing where to start when sharing your faith with others, start with this verse. Memorize it, share it, and use it as an outline for witnessing to others, because it's a powerful summary of the life and ministry of Christ.

Reflection

If you had one minute to convey the purpose of Advent, could you do it? Take a moment and write down one paragraph summarizing what Advent means to you.

What kinds of fears keep you from sharing what Christ has done and will do?

Pray God will use this Advent season, this time of remembrance and expectancy, to better familiarize you with the gospel so you can enjoy it in all its fullness, as well as share it with others in all its glory and grace.

Day 5

*He will be great and will be called the
Son of the Most High. And the Lord God
will give to him the throne of his father
David.* —Luke 1:32

*H*ave you ever known a child prodigy?
One famous example is Pablo Picasso,
who reportedly was painting before he
learned to speak and had surpassed his father's
artistic skills when he was still a child. By the
end of his life, Picasso had produced more than
22,000 works of art that sell for millions of dol-
lars today.

Read Luke 1:32–33. These verses record the
words the angel Gabriel delivered to Mary.

Imagine the anticipation that fills an expecting mother. Now, multiply that sense of anticipation by a thousand, and you might have a glimpse of what Mary must have experienced. Gabriel didn't simply tell Mary she would give birth as a virgin, which was amazing in and of itself, he revealed she would give birth to the Son of the Most High, indicating Jesus would be the Son of God and not simply Mary's child.

Gabriel revealed Jesus would possess the throne of David and reign forever, pointing to the fact the child Mary carried would be the long-awaited Messiah. Have there ever been greater expectations put on a child? Consider child prodigies again for a moment. Prodigies garner so much attention because they achieve in their early years what many adults never achieve in a lifetime. Some graduate college as young teens. Others, as children, paint master-pieces and compose symphonies. They all seem destined for greatness. Unfortunately, not every prodigy is a Picasso. Sometimes child prodigies never quite achieve the level of greatness their younger years seemed to promise. Jesus, though, achieved the greatness He was destined for, perfectly accomplishing the task for which He was sent. Advent season is a time for us to put ourselves in Mary's shoes to reflect on Christ's birth and anticipate His unending reign—just as she surely did upon hearing news from Gabriel of what was to come.

Reflection

Have you ever felt overwhelmed because of people's expectations? What effects did this have on you?

How can remembering Christ's great power and His eternal reign free you from the pressures of the world's expectations?

Why is it important to understand and remember the kinds of expectations that were put on the Messiah?

Day 6

The shepherds said to one another, "Let us go over to Bethlehem and see this thing that has happened, which the Lord has made known to us." —Luke 2:15

On the evening of April 18, 1775, Paul Revere borrowed a horse and set off on his famous midnight ride to warn fellow patriots and colonial militias, the "Redcoats are coming!" British troops were on the move and planned to arrest patriot leaders Samuel Adams and John Hancock, as well as seize colonial military weapons. Revere crossed a river, avoided detection by a British warship, and traveled approximately twenty miles throughout the night. In doing so, history has recorded him as one of the most celebrated Americans of the Revolutionary War.

Read Luke 2:15–16. In the verses preceding this passage, angels delivered news of the arrival of the Messiah to the shepherds. Notice the shepherds responded immediately. They did not take time before setting out. They did not stop for coffee along the way. They did not show up after Jesus grew into a toddler or adolescent. They left in a *hurry* and went straight to Jesus, arriving to see firsthand the scene the angels had described: the baby Jesus lying in a manger. The shepherds recognized the importance of that moment, one God graciously allowed them to share in.

When Paul Revere arrived at the house where Samuel Adams and John Hancock were staying, a guard told him to stop making so much noise. Can you believe that? On the eve of the Revolutionary War, with British troops on their way to capture Adams and Hancock, this guard told Revere to keep it down. Thankfully, though, Revere was undeterred in his urgency and continued alerting people of the British troops' movement. Similarly, the shepherds understood they were being allowed to share in a pivotal moment with Mary, Joseph, and the angels of heaven. We too get to share this moment during Advent as we look back at this breathtaking scene.

Reflection

When have you felt God calling you to something but you hesitated and missed out?

What stopped you from seizing the opportunity God invited you into?

This Advent, don't drag your feet. Like the shepherds, be urgent and deliberate in your movements toward Christ. Pray God will help you be intentional and faithful as you remember the surprising simplicity of Christ's entrance into the world and anticipate His glorious return.

Day 7

Behold, the virgin shall conceive and
bear a son. —Matthew 1:23

Sometimes parents name their newborn baby after a family member. Other times parents might name their child after a favorite celebrity. Whatever the case, in many instances, naming a child can prove to be a difficult task. That's why countless books containing baby names have flooded the market. Sometimes, parents struggling with a name leave it to a vote. Recently, the government of the United Kingdom even created an online poll for citizens to vote for the name of a new polar research vessel. After hundreds of thousands of votes, the name the majority of people voted for was *RRS Boaty McBoatface.*

Read Matthew 1:21*b*–23. An angel appeared to Joseph in a dream and instructed him to name his stepson Jesus, which means, "Jehovah is salvation," or, "the salvation of Yahweh." Jesus is not a common name nowadays, at least not in the United States. Many of us see it as a sacred name. But in the first century, Jesus was not a rare name. In fact, when Jesus was on trial before His crucifixion, Pilate asked the people whether he should release the robber "Jesus Barabbas" or "Jesus who is called the Messiah." Our Savior was not the only person on the block named Jesus, but He was the only one who perfectly embodied that name. He manifested the message of His name by saving us, His people, from our sins.

While some people don't consider the naming process an important one, God chose to make the naming of His Son central to His Son's mission. So He sent an angel to deliver the message. Unlike every other Jesus in the world at the time, Christ alone was miraculously born of a virgin. He alone saved us from our sins. He alone could be called Immanuel, "God with us." Generation after generation of God's people waited anxiously for the coming Messiah. Hundreds of years passed between the time when the prophecies were first announced and the eventual birth of Christ. We are blessed to be where we are on the timeline because we know His name and His ministry, as well as the riches of His salvation.

Reflection

When was a time when you felt the most alone? What type of feelings accompanied the loneliness?

What are some moments in life when you most need to be reminded that Jesus is Immanuel . . . that He is God with us?

The Father chose Jesus' name deliberately. Jesus is our salvation. Jesus is God with us. Pray and ask the Father to remind you this Advent season of the realities of who Jesus is.

Day 8

The people who walked in darkness have seen a great light; those who dwelt in a land of deep darkness, on them has light shone. —Isaiah 9:2

In 2013, a tugboat was capsized by a rogue wave off the coast of Nigeria. The vessel quickly sank to the bottom of the ocean floor. Of the twelve-man crew, only the cook, Harrison Okene, survived by finding a pocket of air inside the overturned ship. Without food or water, Okene was in constant danger of sharks, hypothermia from the frigid ocean temperatures, and carbon dioxide poisoning from the dwindling supply of oxygen in his air pocket.

He spent more than two days at the bottom of the ocean, praying to God and reciting psalms to himself. Miraculously, after being trapped for sixty hours, Okene was finally rescued by a diver searching the sunken ship. When the diver suddenly saw a hand waving to him in the murky ocean waters, he grabbed Okene's hand and came up into the air pocket, the light from his dive helmet shining in Okene's bewildered face.

Read Isaiah 9:1–5. Isaiah prophesied two important events in these verses: the Assyrian invasion of Judah and the coming of the Messiah. For the Israelites, Assyria's invasion of the Promised Land would be a painful experience. However, Isaiah's message was not entirely doom and gloom. He foretold that there would be a great light that would shine on those who live in darkness. This light was a reference to the Messiah, the one who would come and bring gladness to His people. The gladness He brought was like the gladness experienced at harvest, when all the waiting and reaping finally brought life-giving fruit. The kind of gladness the Messiah would bring would also be like the gladness that accompanied triumph in battle, as when an oppressor had finally been defeated and the victory celebration had begun.

Can you imagine the darkness Harrison Okene endured stranded alone at the bottom of the ocean? He did not lose hope though. He prayed to God and leaned on Scripture. After sixty hours, he saw a great light. This light was attached to the helmet of a rescue diver coming to take him home to his family. We too have seen a great light, a light belonging to our rescuer, the Messiah. He came into this world as a human to bring light, victory, and a harvest of righteousness to every man and woman living in darkness.

Reflection

What comes to mind when you think about the light that Jesus brings to a person's life?

Why is it important that our great light, Jesus Christ, came to us as a man?

Have you ever used the excuse, "I'm only human"? Pray and ask God to help you overcome the "I'm only human" excuse as you remember all Jesus accomplished while being both fully God and fully man.

Day 9

For to us a child is born, to us a son is given; and the government shall be upon his shoulder, and his name shall be called Wonderful Counselor, Mighty God, Everlasting Father, Prince of Peace.

—Isaiah 9:6

There is an idea in physics that the universe is expanding in every direction, always getting bigger, called the expanding universe theory. It is held by some that one day the universe will snap back in on itself, like a rubber band pulled too tight and released.

Read Isaiah 9:6–7. This passage opens with a central truth of the gospel: Jesus came as a man. More specifically, He came as a baby. Throughout history, heresies have denied the divinity of Christ while other heresies have rejected His humanity. These verses rebut both heresies by asserting both His humanity (born as a child) and His divinity (Mighty God, Eternal Father).

Consider the power and depth of these words, "to us a son is given." God's Son was given when He came from heaven to earth as a baby. He was given as a leader, a teacher, and a provider. However, in the greatest sense, the Son was given as a sacrifice on the Cross for our atonement—the ultimate expression of God's love.

He is wonderful, a source of joy and delight beyond our understanding. He is our counselor, giving guidance and support through every season of our lives. He is mighty, with power beyond limit or contestation. He is God! He is even called Eternal Father to express His unique oneness with the Father. He is the Prince of Peace and reigns in power and peace forever.

Like the expanding universe theory that says the entire universe with all its stars and worlds is reaching further and further out, our Lord's reign of righteousness extends in every direction. It will go on forever. And unlike the universe, His kingdom will never recede or snap back in on itself. It will go on ceaselessly. Our Lord's rule will have no end.

Reflection

The Son of God was given to us. Take time to meditate on the magnitude and importance of such a statement. Take time to thank God for this profound truth that is sometimes so easy to take for granted.

Today's passage presented us with some of the Lord's names. What names come to mind when you think about Christ?

The world and its desires are passing away, but the kingdom of Christ will have no end. In what ways does this truth inform your everyday decisions?

Day 10

For nothing will be impossible with God.
—Luke 1:37

There have been reports of people displaying superhuman strength, sometimes known as hysterical strength, such as a person lifting a car off someone trapped underneath. One news story reported of a mom who fought off a polar bear to save three children. Hysterical strength supposedly works like this: people find themselves in life-or-death situations and their adrenaline kicks in, giving more energy to their muscles, and enabling them to achieve what seems to be impossible.

Read Luke 1:34–38. Today's passage reminds us that God is the source of all life. As David noted in Psalm 139:13, God is responsible for forming us in our mothers' wombs. Today's passage is a dramatic reminder of this simple truth. By the power of the Most High, a virgin named Mary would give birth to the Son of God and an elderly, barren woman named Elizabeth would give birth to the prophet John the Baptist.

Upon hearing Gabriel's message from God, Mary displayed great faith. She called herself a servant of the Lord and proclaimed, "Let it be to me according to your word" (Luke 1:38). She didn't complain about her circumstances or argue, "Why me?" She considered herself a servant of God and wholeheartedly agreed to God's arrangement, placing her faith fully in His plan. There would certainly be gossip about where her child came from. Undoubtedly, there would be accusations of adultery, which at that time and place in history could have led to a death sentence. But Mary hoped in the Lord.

We have limitations. We can only push ourselves so far. When people push themselves beyond average human ability, such as in moments of hysterical strength, they make the

29

news. But nothing is impossible with God. There is no car He can't lift, so to speak. This is a truth that became very real and personal for Mary in today's passage. Mary knew a couple of facts for certain. First, she was a virgin. Second, virgins can't become pregnant. However, she knew a third fact to be true as well—that nothing is impossible with God.

Reflection

What "impossible" odds are you currently up against in your own life?

In what ways have you either experienced first-hand or heard of God doing the impossible?

There are no "main characters" who receive the lion's share of God's attention. We all share in His love and attention. Thank Him for taking notice of your circumstances and pray He will give you hope as you rest in His power.

Day 11

And this will be a sign for you: you will find a baby wrapped in swaddling cloths and lying in a manger. —Luke 2:12

*A*long with his height (he was the tallest president in the country's history at 6′4″) and his iconic top hat, President Lincoln is perhaps best known for the Emancipation Proclamation and his work to abolish slavery. Lincoln's upbringing has also become the stuff of legend. Although he reached the highest and most respected office in United States government, Lincoln was born in a one-bedroom cabin to poor farmers. Lincoln's parents were uneducated, and with only a year and a half of formal education, Lincoln educated himself by reading every book he could get his hands on. He even taught himself law and became a lawyer before eventually taking the presidency.

Read Luke 2:10–14. The text says the angel brought good news. In the Greek, this is the same word for *gospel*. The angel of the Lord brought the gospel to the shepherds! Biblical commentators have pointed out the angel did not say another prophet or another king had been born. Rather, the angel announced the Lord and Messiah, whom the people of God had long awaited, had finally arrived. Notice there wasn't even a question as to whether the shepherds would go and seek out the Messiah. The angel delivered the news and then immediately provided directions. Their sign would be a baby in a manger. This child was not a mile-marker on their journey to meet the Lord. The shepherds were not supposed to come to the manger for the rest of the directions to the Savior. There in the manger, where least expected, the Messiah had finally arrived.

We enjoy stories of people who came from nothing and rise to greatness. President Lincoln's story possesses this rags-to-riches quality, and it is one of the many things that endear him to Americans to this day. However, there is no greater example of rising from humble beginnings in the history of humankind than the story of the Messiah. Is there a more humble, vulnerable picture than a newborn child lying in a feeding trough? The Lord did not come to earth as an impenetrable warrior conquering kingdoms on horseback. He came quietly, fully God, but born fully human as well, with no one present at His birth besides Mary and Joseph.

Reflection

What elements of Jesus' birth amaze you most? When has the Lord surprised you? How did you respond?

How would you explain to someone who doesn't know Jesus that He was both fully God and fully man?

Circumstances do not hinder God. No matter what your beginnings, He can equip you to serve His people and His gospel.

Day 12

And the child grew and became strong in spirit, and he was in the wilderness until the day of his public appearance to Israel.
—Luke 1:80

One of the greatest powers the earth has ever seen was undoubtedly the Mongol Empire. The Empire existed during the thirteenth and fourteenth centuries, covered 9.15 million miles (that's more than 16 percent of the earth's landmass), and, at its height, had more than 110 million people (that was more than 25 percent of the earth's population at the time). If there was ever a power that seemed insurmountable—an empire that seemed too big to fail—it was the Mongol Empire. Yet, despite its great power and influence, the Mongol Empire only lasted about 160 years. In large part, its loss of dominance was due to the Black Death, a plague that killed anywhere from 50 to 200 million people. In fact, human history has yet to see a government, no matter how big and powerful, stand the test of time.

Read Luke 1:80. Did Jesus *have* to be born a child? Could God have simply sent Jesus, in all of His bright-shining, all-powerful divinity, to immediately take the throne? Sure, God *could have* chosen to do that. However, as is shown throughout the rest of Scripture, we *needed* Jesus to be born a man so He could relate to our weaknesses, share our trials, and absorb God's wrath on the Cross on our behalf. Jesus was born as a human and grew to adulthood as does any child. But He is so much more. He is God the Son, a part of the Triune God, which is why we can call Him Mighty God and Eternal Father. Like those who waited for the Messiah, we also eagerly wait for the day when our Wonderful Counselor and Prince of Peace returns, establishes His government, and rules in peace forever.

The Mongol Empire was the largest contiguous empire of all time, but it did not survive even two hundred years. Even the Roman Empire, which is celebrated as the longest lasting empire of all time, eventually fell. Today Rome hosts tourists instead of conquering lands. The government of Christ, however, will have no end. Since we have nothing in human history to compare this to, it's difficult to wrap our minds around this reality. But consider this: Although all the empires and man-made governments throughout history have had to fight in order to maintain their power, Christ's rule will be maintained in peace for eternity. There is no plague, revolt, or invasion that will overthrow His eternal kingdom.

Reflection

What earthly powers are you in awe of? What impresses you about them?

Why do you think people tend to give more of their awe and attention to earthly governments than to Christ's kingdom?

Our lives can be eternally altered when we embrace Christ. Take time every day to remember the kingdom Christ is establishing.

Day 13

And all who heard it wondered at what the shepherds told them. —Luke 2:18

ave you ever printed off a research paper for school, read a book, or hung a poster on your bedroom wall? If so, then you owe your thanks to Johann Gutenberg, the inventor of the printing press. Before the printing press, books and drawings had to be written and drawn *by hand*. As you can imagine, this process sometimes took a frustratingly long time, and for that reason, not many people had the luxury of owning books and other printed materials. After the invention of the printing press, however, pamphlets, flyers, and books could be produced much faster and more cheaply than the handwritten resources from the past. As a result, information and ideas spread faster than ever.

Read Luke 2:17–20. The angel of the Lord told the shepherds the good news about the birth of Christ. The shepherds saw the Lord in the manger with their own eyes, and then the shepherds spread the good news. Their go-and-tell response is worth our imitation. The surest sign that a person has not truly understood the gospel or has not been moved by its message is a persistent refusal or reluctance to make known to others what he or she has heard, witnessed, and experienced. The shepherds saw the Lord as a baby lying in a manger, and they left preaching the gospel and glorifying God. Our behavior should look similar, especially in light of the Advent season as we reflect on Christ's sacrifice on the Cross, His empty tomb, and His nearing return.

The printing press made the dissemination of news and information quick and less expensive. However, nothing is as effective at stimulating the spread of news like an encounter with Christ. The Apostle Paul, for instance, encountered

Christ on the road to Damascus and took the gospel throughout much of the known world. We can learn from both Mary's quiet introspection and the shepherd's outward celebration and evangelism. Like Mary, we must reflect on this good news inwardly. And, like the shepherds, we must also reflect this good news outwardly to the world around us.

Reflection

Do you have more difficulty with quietly meditating on the gospel or outwardly spreading the gospel? Why?

Today's passage calls us to remember Christ and anticipate His return, as well as to go and tell the good news. Who in your life needs to hear the good news about the Child born to Mary?

Take time now to imitate Mary. Reflect on the incredible reality of Christ's birth. Ask God to open your mind so you can appreciate the grace and wonder of this miracle more fully.

Day 14

*For that which is conceived in her is from
the Holy Spirit. She will bear a son.*
—Matthew 1:20–21

Throughout history, many have credited
dreams for sparking the ideas that lead
to breakthroughs in such areas as lit-
erature, art, and science. Author Mary Shelley
wrote the classic novel *Frankenstein* after being
inspired by a dream. James Weston envisioned
the double helix structure of DNA in a dream.
Elias Howe invented the sewing machine in
1845 after a dream helped him visualize a new
design for the sewing needle. Dreams have

inspired bestselling books, hit songs, and scientific breakthroughs and inventions.

Read Matthew 1:18–21a. In first-century Jewish culture, a betrothal was a binding arrangement that could only be broken by the act of divorce. This is why verse 18 states Mary and Joseph "had been betrothed," while verse 19 refers to Joseph as Mary's husband. Even before the official marriage took place, the couple was already considered husband and wife. Joseph was a good man, and he understood the public stigma associated with divorce. Therefore he planned to divorce Mary quietly, because "before they came together she was found to be with child." However, God sent His angel to deliver a message to Joseph in a dream. Notice God did not send His angel to ask Joseph if he would participate in the plan. Rather, an angel of the Lord explained the situation to Joseph and told Joseph the part he would play.

Inventors and scientists wrestle with mental blocks in their efforts to make the next great discovery. Authors and musicians wrestle with creative blocks in their efforts to write the next great novel or hit song. Often, these breakthroughs come when people are resting from their work, through their dreams when their consciousness is turned off. This was true in the case of Joseph as he wrestled with how to handle Mary's pregnancy. However, it was not Joseph's subconscious speaking to him. Rather, this was an angel of the Lord, a messenger of the living God.

Reflection

In what ways might we make ourselves more sensitive to the voice of God so that, like Joseph, we can live according to His plans rather than culture's expectations?

When have you had in mind to do one thing but God compelled you to do something else? How did this experience teach you to trust Him more?

Lift up a prayer asking God to make you sensitive to His voice so that whenever He has a message for you, you're ready and willing to listen and obey.

Day 15

Behold, your king is coming to you;
righteous and having salvation is he,
humble and mounted on a donkey, even
on a colt, the foal of a donkey.
—Zechariah 9:9

In ancient times, and even some societies today, horses were not simply enjoyed as pets or farm animals. They were seen as labor animals, forms of transportation, and even weapons of war. A warhorse had to be well trained and fearless because it was often called upon to charge heedlessly into heavily armed enemy lines. These horses were known— surprise, surprise—as "chargers." Probably the most famous warhorse in history is the stallion Bucephalus, the horse Alexander the Great rode into every battle.

Read Zechariah 9:9–10. Our King is humble and peace loving, "righteous and having salvation." Matthew 21 recounts the fulfillment of today's passage when Jesus rode into Jerusalem, the city of His execution, on a donkey. As we know, He did not come riding a warhorse like Alexander the Great to conquer and overthrow governments as some expected of the Messiah. Instead, He entered Jerusalem with the very same intentions with which He entered the world as a child born in a manger—to bring redemption through His sacrifice on the Cross. Our Lord, worthy of all worship and praise, took the nature of a servant. The same is expected of each of us.

As Christ entered the city on a donkey, the people rejoiced with shouts of "Hosanna," which means, "Save now!" Our Lord brought salvation in His first coming, and He will conquer all evil once and for all time in His second coming. While the gospel is continuing to spread around the globe, war and sin persist. However, to our great joy, there will come a day when our Lord returns, banishes sin, and rules in peace forever.

Reflection

Many people questioned Jesus' tactics. They wanted Him conquering kingdoms on a warhorse rather than entering peacefully on a donkey. When have you found yourself questioning God's methods?

How did you work your way through that questioning (such as through prayer, Scripture, or the help of a mentor)?

Take time now to thank the Lord for being both just *and* humble, for bringing salvation instead of condemnation, for riding peacefully on a colt rather than on a warhorse. Ask Him to help you trust Him, especially when you don't understand His ways. When you find yourself confused by His methods, remember the salvation He brought and the joys of that great gift.

Day 16

He was despised and rejected by men,
a man of sorrows and acquainted with
grief; and as one from whom men hide
their faces he was despised, and we
esteemed him not. —Isaiah 53:3

A study conducted by Rice University found that attractive people are generally trusted more. The researchers called this a "beauty premium," meaning that even when we don't know someone personally, if he or she is attractive, then we're likely to assume they have more intelligence and greater leadership skills than others. Believe it or not, this bias has made its way into our presidential races.

The first televised US presidential debate was in 1960 between John F. Kennedy and Richard Nixon. After the debate, viewers said Kennedy appeared handsome and confident, while Nixon appeared sweaty and pale. It is widely believed today that Kennedy's beauty premium marked a turning point in his campaign and helped him win the presidency.

Read Isaiah 53:1–4. In this passage, Isaiah gave one of the most vivid pictures of Christ we have in all of the messianic prophecies of the Old Testament. Interestingly, Isaiah did not paint a picture of a physically imposing, handsome man. However, he didn't describe the Messiah as hideous either. Instead, Isaiah described a man of average appearances, without the charms of good looks or the benefits of physical beauty. Further, Isaiah foretold that Jesus would be a man of sorrows. Elsewhere in Scripture is documented that Jesus experienced every temptation and hardship we face. This is what makes Him our great High Priest who is able to personally relate with our struggles.

Jesus came to us without the beauty premium. He wasn't interested in gaining people's trust using the advantages of good looks. Instead,

Jesus came with a central mission in mind: to bear our grief and sorrows and endure God's wrath against sin on our behalf. While appearances have their advantages if you're trying to get ahead or run for president, Jesus didn't come to get ahead. He came to serve people. When it comes to salvation, the beauty premium carries no weight.

Reflection

Have you ever witnessed the beauty premium play out in real life? Describe the experience.

In what ways might this passage from Isaiah teach us to look at people differently?

Consider the sorrows you have experienced so far. Take some time now to thank the Lord for His willingness to experience every grief we experience and for taking up our sorrows as His own.

Day 17

The blind receive their sight and the lame walk, lepers are cleansed and the deaf hear, and the dead are raised up, and the poor have good news preached to them.
—Matthew 11:5

e live in the age of information. The answers to our questions about history, science, math, and popular culture are readily available with a quick web search. And we can send information as quickly as we can access it. We can email. We can text. We can tweet. We can video chat. We can call. The point is we live in a world in which we can send and receive information at the touch of a button. However, sometimes these systems don't work. Sometimes we need to access information on the Internet, but our Wi-Fi is down. Sometimes we need to ask someone an important question, but they aren't answering the phone or responding to texts. And because of the general ease of accessing information, we are also becoming increasingly impatient. We want our answers now, and we have no patience for slow Internet access.

Read Matthew 11:2–6. John the Baptist was imprisoned for rebuking King Herod, who had married his own brother's wife. Try to imagine the sense of confusion, loneliness, and doubt John must have experienced after being thrown into a dungeon for doing what was morally right. John was understandably struggling in his difficult circumstances and sent his disciples to Jesus, probably in hopes of receiving confirmation that his faith had not been misplaced. However difficult it might have been for John in that dungeon, rest assured that when he received Jesus' response, he was refreshed and strengthened. His disciples brought back a message from Jesus that painted a picture of the Messiah serving His people. Yes, John had been unfairly imprisoned, but he also had confidence that he had put his hope in the true Messiah, the Expected One.

If we were in John the Baptist's position, we would face many of the difficult emotions he likely faced. However, we might also find ourselves facing the unique challenge of impatience. We have been trained to expect solutions to arrive quickly, whether from a Google search or a fast food drive-through window. Something we might learn from Advent, as well as from today's passage, is the important role of patience in our faith. Our Lord became a servant, and He still serves today. Our Lord performed miracles, and He still does so today. We must be patient, though, trusting in His timing as we enjoy Him now and await His return.

Reflection

When has your faith been tested? In what ways did the Lord prove Himself faithful in that difficult situation?

When was a time when you took the good news of Jesus to someone who, like John the Baptist, was struggling? How did he or she respond?

Accepting Christ as our Savior changes our lives. Consider how our lives can change even more if we take steps to emulate the servant heart of Christ.

Day 18

The Lᴏʀᴅ God has opened my ear,
and I was not rebellious;
I turned not backward. —Isaiah 50:5

tudies have shown that many young people use social media to achieve a sense of worth. In fact, in some cases, young people feel that the number of likes, comments, and retweets they receive is a direct reflection of how highly they're valued and how much they're loved. Maybe you can relate. Perhaps you've posted a photo or video to social media that didn't receive enough likes or comments, so you took it down because it made you feel overlooked or unimportant. Research has found that one of the reasons we value social media comments and likes is because this online approval triggers an increase of dopamine in the body, the chemical that makes us feel happy. This feeling of happiness keeps us seeking the online approval of others, publicizing the best versions of ourselves to strengthen our online image.

Read Isaiah 50:4–5. These verses are prophetically spoken from the point of view of the Messiah. In the New American Standard Bible, the Father gave Christ "the tongue of disciples" (some Bible versions translate this as the tongue of the *learned*, *taught*, or *experienced*), indicating that Jesus spoke to His followers with perfect wisdom and insight. Notice, however, that Jesus didn't use His deep knowledge and gift for oratory to make a name for Himself or climb social ladders. Rather, as seen in the Gospel accounts of His ministry, Jesus used His words to unburden people, free minds from the lies they had learned from false religions, and draw weary hearts closer to the Living God.

It has become common practice for people to share polished scenes of their lives on social media to impress others. Of course, there's nothing inherently wrong with being active on social media, but the trouble comes when we rely on the likes and comments to make us feel valued. In contrast, Jesus took His life, all of His power and knowledge, and used it to sustain weary people. You see, while we often use what we have to impress others and feel important, Jesus used what He had to serve the weary in perfect obedience to the Father (v. 5). To this day, Jesus uses what He has to serve us.

Reflection

Why do so many of us seek the approval of others?

Why do you think people generally find it more difficult to serve rather than be served?

Consider ways in which you follow Jesus' example, taking steps to serve others rather than seeking the approval of strangers. Keeping focus on Him is a far more worthy goal.

Day 19

*But emptied himself, by taking the form
of a servant, being born in the likeness
of men.* —Philippians 2:7

*U*nderstandably, *slavery* is a word that conjures up a lot of strong emotions. The unfortunate truth is that no matter how far back in history you go, no matter the culture or nationality you investigate, you will likely find slavery existed in some form or fashion. The Egyptians notoriously used slave labor to build their iconic pyramids. The Nazis used slave labor to produce supplies for their troops during World War II. In the United States, slaves were forced to work in tobacco, rice, and cotton fields from the seventeenth century until late into the nineteenth century. Tragically, slavery still exists around the world, from the labor camps of North Korea to the sweatshops of Asia and beyond.

Read Philippians 2:5–8. This passage is a concise, perfectly distilled picture of the gospel. Jesus is God who became a man in order to become our stand-in and absorb the punishment for our sins on our behalf. The words *servant* and *slave* are often translated "bond servant" when describing Jesus and the nature of His work. The significance of this phrase to our theology can't be overstated. Yes, it's important to understand that Jesus is God, but even demons understand that. Yes, it's important to understand that Jesus died on the Cross, but even the demons understand that. We must understand *why* He did what He did and what He accomplished in taking on the role of a servant. Then we must respond in kind by becoming bond servants of the Lord.

As bond servants of Christ, we follow Him and serve Him, not because we're *forced* to do so, and not because He *needs* us to labor on His behalf, but because we *choose* to do so in faith.

Because, although Jesus is God, He took on the form of a bond servant and bought our freedom at the price of His own life.

Reflection

When you think about Jesus in the role of a servant, what stories from Scripture come to mind?

What excuses do you think people generally use when deciding not to serve others?

Remember how different our faith and lives would be today if Jesus chose to make excuses rather than choosing to take on the form of a bond servant. Choosing to serve others opens our hearts and minds to the way of Christ and shows us the desperate need others have for compassion and love.

Day 20

And going into the house, they saw the child with Mary his mother, and they fell down and worshiped him. Then, opening their treasures, they offered him gifts, gold and frankincense and myrrh.

—Matthew 2:11

*W*hile celebrities are no strangers to receiving all kinds of gifts from their fans, sometimes these gifts can be strange, or even downright disturbing. The Jonas Brothers once received a dead shark from a fan. Taylor Swift received a turtle shell with her face painted on it. In the 1970s, country music star Dolly Parton was given a baby. Yes, a baby!

A fan actually left her child outside the gate to Parton's home. Presidents have also received their fair share of odd gifts over the years. Theodore Roosevelt received a zebra and a lion, and Richard Nixon was given a panda.

Read Matthew 2:11–12. It is believed that these magi (or wise men, as some translations refer to them) were likely astronomers, men who studied the stars. This would make sense, considering the magi followed a light in the sky to find their way to Jesus. It has been asserted by many theologians that the gifts brought by the magi had special meaning. The gold represented Christ's royalty, the frankincense represented His divinity (because incense was used by priests throughout the Old Testament), and myrrh represented His death (because myrrh was used during Jesus' burial). The magi didn't stop at bringing Christ material things, though. As we see in verse 11, they also brought Him their worship.

In our own culture, it is common for people to bring gifts when meeting someone of great importance—whether it's a fan handing a favorite actor a painstakingly drawn sketch or a foreign dignitary giving the president a jewel encrusted sword. The magi gave evidence they were journeying to someone infinitely more important than a celebrity or a president—by their gifts and their act of falling to the ground to worship Him. This Advent season, as you reflect on Christ's sacrifice, follow the example of the magi and continue to surrender more of yourself to the Lord, laying down all of your life and all of your worship.

Reflection

What are the kinds of gifts that mean the most to you (such as expensive gifts, handmade gifts, or rare gifts)? Explain.

Pause for a moment and think about the gifts the magi brought to Jesus. What made these gifts so special?

Consider how you can imitate the behavior of the magi in your day-to-day life. Ask God to help you surrender everything you hold dear at the feet of Jesus, holding nothing back as you remember His sacrifice.

Day 21

*And leaving Nazareth he went and lived
in Capernaum by the sea, in the territory
of Zebulun and Naphtali, so that what
was spoken by the prophet Isaiah might
be fulfilled.* —Matthew 4:13–14

laska is the northernmost state in the
US, and certain parts of the state experience long periods of darkness—some of
which can last up to two months. This has led to
approximately a fifth of the population in Alaska
suffering from seasonal affective disorder,
which is a form of depression caused by a lack of
light. In fact, people miss the sunlight so much

there have been reports of flights to Hawaii in the winter selling out a year in advance.

Read Matthew 4:12–16. This reference to the prophecy of Isaiah about the coming Messiah also spoke to events during Isaiah's time as well as those in the future. Isaiah's prophecy pointed to the future invasion of the Assyrians, which was the great darkness that God's people would have to endure. However, the prophecy wasn't all doom and gloom. Isaiah also spoke of a great light.

This great light was the arrival of the promised Messiah, the awaited Savior, the conquering Lord, Jesus Christ. The people of God would wait approximately seven hundred years before the arrival of the promised Messiah of Isaiah's prophecies, but His arrival was like the joy of the harvest, which represented life and was the culmination of difficult sowing, and like the joys of dividing spoils, which represented victory after a tough and long-fought battle.

Alaskan residents have been affected by long periods of uninterrupted night. Yet they know in the midst of this darkness the light will return in summer. In fact, in the northernmost areas of Alaska where the winter darkness lasts the longest, they also experience the longest stretches of uninterrupted sunlight, sometimes lasting nearly three months.

Ultimately, the Lord will deliver peace. Although we might be surrounded by darkness, He brings the light of His presence into our hearts and minds.

Reflection

What moments of darkness have you recently endured or are currently enduring?

In what ways do you reflect the great light of Christ to others?

Ask God to stir up your affections for the greatest wonder of all: the arrival and the work of Jesus Christ, the Son of God, in this world. Pray for His peace and light to spread to others through you.

Day 22

*I am the LORD; I have called you
in righteousness; I will take you by
the hand and keep you; I will give you
as a covenant for the people,
a light for the nations.* —Isaiah 42:6

In 2010, a group of Chilean miners faced possible death when a cave-in left them trapped two thousand feet underground. Over the course of sixty-nine days, they survived on limited food and water. By the time they were rescued, each miner had lost an average of eighteen pounds. Don Jose, who was nicknamed The Pastor, has been celebrated for helping keep morale high during the miners' difficult ordeal.

Don Jose's actual pastor said Jose knew Scripture so well he was able to preach the Word to his companions while trapped in the mine, despite the fact he didn't have a Bible with him. Jose led the miners in devotions twice a day, and by the end of their harrowing experience, approximately twenty miners reported they had put their faith in Christ. The Pastor helped to deliver hope and light in an emotionally, spiritually, and literally dark situation.

Read Isaiah 42:1–7. The servant in this passage is a clear reference to Jesus. Jesus, the Messiah, is the Servant who gives us life, and He is also the Servant who gives us a pattern to live by. Our Lord, who astoundingly serves *us*, has also called us to serve Him and to serve others by following His example. We must care for justice as He cares for justice. We must live in righteousness and call others to righteousness, just as He does. We must be a light to those in darkness, just as He is the Light. As our Light, Jesus guides us out of the darkness of sin and selfishness. As our Light, Jesus leads us in the paths of righteousness. Ultimately, as the "Light to the nations," Jesus delivers hope and a future to people of every nation by making a way for us to be saved through His sacrifice.

After news began circulating about life inside the mine during those two long, dark months, many people began calling Don Jose a hero. In an interview, he was quick to give credit where credit was due. "The true hero is Jesus Christ," he asserted. "He is the one that deserves honor and glory." Of course, Jose is 100 percent correct. Jose preached the Word within the darkness of the collapsed mine, and in doing so he helped bring light into a dark situation. However, to an incalculably greater extent, Jesus brought light to our darkness when He stepped *into* our darkness, lowered Himself into the hopelessness of our situation, and lit our way to freedom.

Reflection

What is one area of your life that needs more light?

What kind of comfort do you take in knowing there is no darkness, no matter how deep or dark, beyond the reach of Jesus, the Light to the nations?

The gospel has spread far and wide, but there are still corners of the world where the light of Christ has yet to be seen. Pray for those in the darkness, that they will see the Light of the nations and believe.

Day 23

A light for revelation to the Gentiles, and for glory to your people Israel. —Luke 2:32

Martin Luther was a monk who led the way for the sixteenth century Protestant Reformation with his 95 Theses, a document protesting the Catholic church's practice of selling indulgences for the forgiveness of sins. Essentially, certain leaders within the Catholic church led laypeople to believe if they paid the church they would be exempt from punishment for their sins. In addition to his 95 Theses, Martin Luther also translated the Bible into German so the average believer could have access to the Word of God in a translation other than Latin, a language most Germans couldn't read. Can you imagine what it would be like today if the only version of the Bible available to you was written in Latin?

Read Luke 2:30–32. The words recorded in today's passage were spoken by Simeon, a righteous and devout man who was eagerly awaiting the long-anticipated Messiah. The Holy Spirit had assured Simeon he would not die until he saw the Messiah with his own eyes. For Simeon, setting eyes on Christ was more precious than life. The Spirit led Simeon to the Temple the day Mary and Joseph brought Jesus. Simeon saw the child Jesus there, took Him in his arms, and spoke the words of celebration in verses 30–32. The child Simeon held in his hands was the light of revelation, the hope for salvation for both the Jews and the Gentile outsiders.

The Reformation brought a light of revelation to common people by placing an emphasis on the teachings of the Bible over the traditions of the church and by placing an emphasis on salvation by grace through faith rather than through the purchase of indulgences. In this way, Martin Luther and other reformers followed the example of Christ, who was the first to bring a light of revelation to the people. Simeon waited faithfully for the Messiah, and he was rewarded. He was finally able to see the salvation of God's people with his own eyes and hold the Messiah in his arms! Advent reminds us to be more like Simeon and all the other people of God who faithfully waited for the Messiah. The difference is that we wait for His *second* coming. Like Simeon, when that day comes, we will be rewarded.

Reflection

In what ways has Jesus continued to be a light of revelation in your life since your salvation?

In what ways are you actively sharing the light of revelation with those around you?

Every believer has experienced the light of revelation firsthand—that eureka moment when our eyes see Jesus' salvation. Take a moment to reflect on the Lord's saving work in your own life, and then thank Him for giving light to your life.

Day 24

He says: "It is too light a thing that you
should be my servant to raise up the
tribes of Jacob and to bring back the
preserved of Israel; I will make you as a
light for the nations, that my salvation
may reach to the end of the earth."
—Isaiah 49:6

From 2008 to 2009, New York police officer Adrian Schoolcraft made secret recordings of his fellow officers because he was concerned about misconduct at his precinct. According to Schoolcraft, in order to meet arrest quotas, the officers at his precinct were deliberately arresting innocent people, while also sometimes failing to report serious crimes. When Schoolcraft initially voiced his concerns, he was told to get another job. Things escalated, however, when word got out that he was recording conversations within the precinct. One evening, officers from his precinct arrived at his apartment, handcuffed him to a gurney, and had him forcibly committed to a psychiatric ward. Schoolcraft was eventually released from the hospital and, not so surprisingly, decided to take legal action against his precinct.

Read Isaiah 49:6–7. Isaiah referred to the Messiah as a light to the nations, the One who causes kings to rise and princes to bow, and the light that brings salvation to the people of Israel as well as the people of every nation. Despite the fact that Jesus was the Messiah, the One the people of God had waited for and long anticipated, Isaiah explained that the people of Israel would still reject Him. And that's exactly what they did. The very people He came to save called Him crazy, a liar, and a blasphemer. Jesus was innocent, but He endured mockery, abuse, and eventually death. The day is coming, though, when every knee will bow before

Him and every tongue will confess that Jesus is Lord.

Officer Adrian Schoolcraft was despised by many officers in his precinct for doing the right thing and shedding light on misconduct and corruption. He suffered for doing the right thing and was wrongfully committed to the psych ward of a hospital. He has since received a small slice of vindication in the form of a $600,000 settlement. Similarly, Jesus shed light on our misconduct and our sinful condition. His light, though, is not a condemning spotlight that simply highlights our sins. Rather, it is a guiding light that leads us to the truth, grace, and salvation of the Lord. He was despised and abhorred, but He was vindicated. He was proven right and true when He rose from the dead, and He will be proven right and true once and for all when He returns.

Reflection

Have you ever spoken with someone who despised or abhorred the Lord? If so, what was his or her reasoning? How did you respond?

What sin in your life might the Lord be shedding light on now?

Jesus' light reveals our sins, even the most private misconduct of our lives, the things no one else knows about. Jesus' light also leads us to repentance and salvation. Take a moment and pray for yourself as well as for those around you, asking the Lord to guide them to His grace.

Day 25

*The shepherds returned, glorifying and
praising God for all that they had heard
and seen, as it had been told them.*
—Luke 2:20

*S*occer is the most popular sport in the
world. One of the most entertaining
aspects of the game is watching the goal
celebrations. Since the average game only sees
two to three goals, these celebrations are high
energy and very entertaining, sometimes includ-
ing cartwheels and choreographed dances.
Player Lomana LuaLua even celebrated a goal
with ten consecutive back flips. And it's not just
the players who celebrate. Even the crowd and

the announcers are electric after a goal. In fact, in 2013, a Romanian announcer broke the record for the longest goal shout, yelling "goal" for one minute and eight seconds in a single breath!

Read Luke 2:16–20. The angel who appeared to the shepherds had essentially preached the gospel to them, notifying them of the arrival of the long-awaited Savior. The shepherds wasted no time in making their way to the child. Today's passage recounts the arrival of the shepherds to Jesus' birthplace. Mary and Joseph were no doubt surprised at the presence of strangers arriving to visit their newly born child.

Mary's response was one of quiet introspection as she treasured the good news of the gospel in her heart. The shepherds, on the other hand, left young Jesus, glorifying God and praising Him with outward enthusiasm and passion. People celebrate the gospel in different ways. It is important we realize that one reaction is not better than the other, but no one will walk away from our glorified Lord without giving Him the praise He rightly deserves. Every knee will bow before Him.

Sporting events evoke great excitement from players, fans, and announcers alike. However, the celebration of the gospel is a celebration that will ring throughout eternity. Whereas the world's longest goal shout lasted one minute and eight seconds, the worship and praise rightly belonging to our God will never cease because He will always be worthy of it, and the joy of His gospel will never cease.

Reflection

Do you remember how you felt when you first heard the gospel? How did you react?

What does glorifying God look like in your own life? Who have you told about this?

The shepherds told Mary and Joseph everything they had learned about Jesus. Take a moment and pray for nonbelievers in your life, that the gospel will reroute their lives.

Day 26

And you, O Bethlehem, in the land of Judah, are by no means least among the rulers of Judah; for from you shall come a ruler who will shepherd my people Israel.
—Matthew 2:6

It is not uncommon for a hometown to celebrate one of its own who has gone off to do great things. Soldiers returning home from war, presidents visiting their home states, and celebrities of every kind are accustomed to receiving hometown parades in their honor. People line the streets and wait, sometimes for hours, for the guest of honor to pass by. When they finally arrive, confetti falls while people cheer and take pictures. Super Bowl champs, army generals, and all variety of famous people have received the honor of ticker tape parades upon returning home.

Read Matthew 2:1–6. There is a lot of tradition surrounding the magi. For example, Christmas carols have been written about the three kings who visited the Christ child. However, Scripture says nothing about three kings. What we know for certain is that these visitors were wise men, perhaps astronomers. Additionally, speculation has considered the presence of "His star," as referred to by the magi. Scholars suggest it might have been a comet, an alignment of planets, or perhaps an actual star. Whatever the case, what is important is that the star is referred to as *Christ's* star, because it fulfilled the function of lighting the way to the Lord. Likewise, we too must be Christ's light in the world, leading others to Him.

Consider the magi's reaction to the news of Christ's birth. Upon receiving the news of the Lord's arrival they responded with wholehearted devotion, traveling a great distance to find Him through a journey that would probably have taken several months, if not a couple of years. Once they arrived, the magi were ready to worship the King. Contrast that with Herod's response. He only wanted to find Jesus in order to kill Him.

Similar to the way a state will take pride in identifying itself as the birthplace of a famous person, so too the small town of Bethlehem had its own hometown hero in King David. However, following Jesus' birth, Bethlehem had the even more incredible honor of identifying itself as the birthplace of the Messiah!

Reflection

In what ways can you be more like the star that led the wise men to Christ as you lead those in your life closer to the Lord?

Herod wanted to find Jesus because he saw Him as a threat. Is there someone in your life who views Jesus as a threat? What steps can you take to reach out to him or her?

As Christ followers, our home is with God. We should focus on doing all we can this season— and beyond—to make our heavenly "hometown" proud.

Day 27

Arise, shine, for your light has come, and the glory of the L ORD has risen upon you.
—Isaiah 60:1

In 2003, the Walt Disney Concert Hall was completed in downtown Los Angeles, California. The project took approximately sixteen years to finish at a cost of an estimated $274 million. The building was constructed with shiny stainless steel walls, giving the concert hall an out-of-this-world, almost spaceship appearance. The design was praised by architect enthusiasts, but people who lived and worked in the area weren't as impressed. That's because the stainless steel walls reflected the sunlight so intensely that nearby residents and business owners complained temperatures at their properties were reaching 138 degrees Fahrenheit. The reflections were also blinding people who drove past the concert hall. So, in 2014, the shiny walls were sandblasted to dull the bright reflection.

Read Isaiah 60:1–3. The good news of today's passage is that light has come! Isaiah 59 records that the people of God had endured great darkness and hardships as a result of their sins. Every believer has experienced the dark cloud that sin casts over our lives. We know firsthand the experience of feeling distant from the glory and brightness of the Lord's presence. But at the coming of Jesus, the glory of the Lord returned to His people—a glorious light that will return once and for all at Christ's second coming. The good news for all those living in darkness is Christ came and made the light of God's glory— His presence and power and holiness—available to each of us.

Isaiah 60:1 instructs us to arise and shine. As those enjoying the glorious presence of the Lord, we should also be those who reflect the light and glory of the Lord as dramatically as the Walt Disney Concert Hall, reflecting His light so powerfully that it changes the atmosphere of the rooms we're in and alters the nature of our relationships.

Reflection

Is there anything in your life sandblasting and dulling the light you're reflecting? If so, what steps might you take to ensure the light of the Lord isn't diminished in your life?

Who in your life is currently living in darkness? What are three small, practical things you can do this week to arise and reflect some of the Lord's light into their lives?

Stop and thank the Lord for bringing you out of darkness and sharing His glorious light with you. Pray for those experiencing a deep darkness, and ask the Lord to use you to shine His light into their lives.

Day 28

*Where is he who has been born king of
the Jews? For we saw his star when it
rose and have come to worship him.*
—Matthew 2:2

*U*ndercover Boss is a reality television
show that takes company executives
and puts them in the shoes of average workers. Millions of viewers have tuned
in since it first premiered in 2010 to see what
happens when bosses and company presidents
leave the comforts of their offices and go into
the field to perform the everyday tasks of their
employees. During one episode, the president
of Orkin Pest Control went on the road and

joined his employees in the dirty work of exter-minating cockroaches and ants. And that's why people love the show—a boss left his leather office chair to crawl on his belly under a dirty sink shoulder-to-shoulder with insects and rodents.

Read Matthew 2:1–2. Today's passage men-tions two kings. The first was King Herod, or Herod the Great, a notoriously vicious and cruel man, of whom it was said, "It's better to be Herod's pig than Herod's son." The second was Jesus, King of the Jews. Commentators have noted that "King of the Jews" is a significant title because, while many looked down on the Jews as an unimpressive people, the Lord viewed the Jewish people as a *chosen* people.

The wise men, or magi, searched for Jesus in Jerusalem. Understandably, they expected the King of the Jews to be born somewhere central. Instead of finding Jesus, the King of the Jews, they found King Herod in his opu-lent palace. But Herod was not the king they had traveled to worship. The King they sought had been born in the small, sleepy town of Bethlehem. Martin Luther noted that Jesus had not performed any miracles or preached a single sermon at this point—He was only a baby, after all—and yet He was already making waves in the world, drawing people in with His light and attracting the worship He alone is worthy of.

If you had gone looking for the president of Orkin during the filming of *Undercover Boss*, you wouldn't have found him in his office at the company headquarters. Instead, you would have found him under a sink, working with his employees to exterminate insects. Likewise, Jesus came to earth in the way people least expected—born in a manger, rather than a palace. The wise men learned this firsthand when they went looking for Jesus in Jerusalem. Jesus' humble birth was indicative of His ministry. He did not teach from the comforts of a palace; instead, He walked among His people as a servant and personally brought the light of salvation to the world.

Reflection

How might you follow Jesus' example and surprise people with your service this week?

In what ways can you act as a guiding light in the lives of others, showing them the way to Jesus?

As He did for the wise men, the Lord has provided each of us with guidance and direction, leading us closer and closer to Himself. Thank God for the light He has given to us.

Day 29

But let all who take refuge in you rejoice;
let them ever sing for joy, and spread
your protection over them, that those
who love your name may exult in you.
—Psalm 5:11

There's a great deal of excitement and enthusiasm at concerts. You can feel the ground move beneath your feet and feel the music pulse in your chest. Some concerts have lasted a *long* time. Bruce Springsteen performed a concert in 2012 that lasted more than four hours. In 2014, a number of acts came together in Las Vegas to perform back-to-back over the span of more than *two weeks*.

And as you read this, there are plans to break the record for the longest concert. After it's all said and done, the concert, which will be performed nonstop by an automated organ, will last 639 years!

Read Psalm 5:10–12. The psalmist David referred to "them" as those who persisted in their sin, wickedness, iniquity, bloodshed, and deceit. David beseeched the Lord for His justice *and* His blessing. He asked the Lord to give the wicked over to their wickedness but to give joy and gladness to those who take refuge in Him and sing in the shelter of His mighty wings. Those of us who take shelter in the Lord are not to enjoy the shade of His shelter in silence. We are to sing in His shadows. We are to sing behind the shield of His favor.

We attend concerts and sing songs as a form of expression, as a way of sharing our thoughts and feelings on a collective scale. We sing. The birds sing. Angels sang songs of praise before we existed. And we will sing for joy in a concert that will continue throughout eternity. That is not to say we will sing without ceasing but that the Lord will be our song. We will never grow tired of singing His praises because the joy of the Lord will never weaken in our hearts.

Reflection

Charles Spurgeon once noted, "The ungodly are not half so restrained in their blasphemy as we are in our praise." Do you find it difficult to let out exclamations of joy to the Lord? If so, why do you suppose that is?

What steps can we take to be freer in our worship and more deliberate in our joyful praise of God?

Take time now to praise the Lord. Perhaps you feel like singing. Maybe you feel more inclined to speak out loud to Him. Or you might simply sit in silence and reflect on His greatness.

Day 30

*The L*ORD *said to me, "You are My Son;
today I have begotten you."* —Psalm 2:7

The United States was built on democratic principles, namely the right of people to rule themselves by the power of their vote. Democracy is roughly 2,500 years old and was originally introduced in Ancient Greece. Before then, one person or a select group, based solely on their social or economic status, made decisions in government on behalf of the rest of the population. This opened societies up to a number of injustices. Unfortunately, parts of the world remain in which the citizens don't have a voice in their government.

Read Psalm 2:6–8. We are considered children of God as those created by Him in His image. However, in an even more extravagant sense, we are known as children of God when we place our faith in Christ and receive His Spirit—when we are adopted as members of His family and not simply members of His creation. But no one can call himself a son of God in the unique way that Jesus can call Himself the only begotten Son of God (v. 7). But, "begotten" doesn't mean Christ was created, because there was never a time when He did not exist alongside the Father and the Spirit. Rather, "begotten" indicates the Father and the Son share the same nature.

Jesus was never made, but He *was* sent by the Father to earth and entered the world as a baby born to a virgin. In that sense, our Lord was begotten here on earth. But even entering the scene as a baby, Jesus still carried the divine nature of the Father. The baby born in that manger had no beginning or end. The baby born in that manger was, is, and will forever be the King.

We live in a world in which leaders must be kept accountable by the general population because everyone is prone to sin. This is why democracy is so widely celebrated . . . because it gives a voice to the people. But in God's kingdom, He has the final say, and He rules in righteousness without need of anyone to keep Him accountable. As believers, we have great hope for the day when sin is no more and the Lord rules in love and righteousness forever.

Reflection

What is one area of your life where you need more accountability?

What comforts do you find in knowing that nations and the very ends of the earth are under the authority of Christ?

Pray for those in power, that they will lead like Christ. And pray that God will put people in your life to keep you accountable.

Day 31

I, I am the Lord, and besides me there is no savior. —Isaiah 43:11

*E*ighteen-year-old Malachi Love-Robinson was arrested in early 2016 for impersonating a doctor. Love-Robinson went so far as to hire staff for his fake medical practice and create fake diplomas. The danger of such a scheme is clear, isn't it? Medical care is often a life-or-death issue and is directly correlated with someone's quality of life. That's why doctors must spend, on average, eight to ten years studying before they can practice medicine, why Love-Robinson was arrested for pretending to be something he wasn't, and why the sheriff's office that arrested Love-Robinson released the following statement after his arrest: "Just because you saw a season of *Grey's Anatomy* doesn't mean you could practice medicine."

Read Isaiah 43:10–13. As believers, we are all witnesses. The Hebrew word for *witnesses* is `*ed*, which means "testimony" or "evidence." As those who have experienced the greatness of God personally, and as those who have enjoyed His grace and *witnessed* His power in our own lives, we become God's evidence to the world. We are those who, through our personal testimonies, give evidence of God's existence. We are the evidence that Jesus alone is Lord and Savior; no other gods exist to give credit for the life change we've experienced.

Malachi Love-Robinson was arrested for impersonating a doctor, an act that put people at risk. Anyone or anything other than Jesus that claims to offer salvation is simply an impersonator, offering false gods that put people at risk. Love-Robinson did not have the knowledge or experience necessary to give sick people medical care. Simply put, he didn't have what it takes to save lives. Likewise, the false gods in the world today do not have what it takes to save lives. Jesus alone is Savior because He is the One who came to earth, put on flesh, lived a sinless life, and suffered a criminal's death on our behalf. He has done more than we could have ever asked for. The idols of this world, the impersonators, have done nothing.

Reflection

In the past year, how many opportunities have you taken to act as Christ's witness?

Who in your life needs to hear your testimony? What's prevented you from sharing with them?

Ask God to remove the fears and apprehensions that are keeping you from being His witness to the world. Ask Him to give you wisdom and courage as you share your testimony with others and to preemptively soften their hearts to hear and receive your testimony.

Day 32

> *The whole earth is at rest and quiet;*
> *they break forth into singing.* —Isaiah 14:7

Champion warfare is single combat between two opposing sides' best fighters or champions. An example of this technique is found in Homer's epic poem *Iliad* when fabled warriors Achilles and Hector met on the battlefield. In Greek mythology, Achilles was considered the greatest warrior on earth, and Hector was Troy's prince and its greatest fighter. Generally speaking, in champion warfare, the two best soldiers of opposing sides battle in order to decide which side will be the victor. In the

Iliad, Achilles defeated Hector, which marked the end of Troy.

Read Isaiah 14:4–8. Today's passage pointed to a joyous day when Israel would be free and could rest from their oppressor. The people of Israel were exiles, conquered by Babylon and taken from their homes. In the midst of their oppression, Isaiah delivered God's good news of a future hope. The people of God would one day be free of the power of Babylon. Not only that, but God was going to take away Babylon's power, breaking the staff and scepter of wicked rulers.

Isaiah's words are not just words of hope for God's people from the past. This good news is the joyous inheritance of every believer. We will have rest from the sorrow, bondage, and fear of our sin. The relentless oppression and servitude of sin made slaves of us all. However, our Lord will have the ultimate victory over sin. There is a spiritual war that takes place between good and evil, and between the realm of righteousness and the realm of sin. The Champion of heaven will face off with the champion of hell. Our Champion, our Lord, will put a final end to the oppression of Satan, and his defeat will mark the end of the power of sin.

Peace and celebration follows every victory. This was true of the Israelites' eventual liberation from Babylon, and this will be true of our eventual liberation from the evil of this world. At that time, when the powers of evil are subdued forever in hell and our Champion the Lord brings the new heaven to the new earth, the whole earth will rest and we will have joy eternal.

Reflection

What are your tactics when putting up a fight against sin and its temptations? Who in your life is dealing with pain and turmoil?

How does the hope of Christ's future defeat of Satan make you stronger in your day-to-day life?

Take this time to pray for those around you who are struggling, that they will have rest, quiet, and joy.

Day 33

But we see him who for a little while was made lower than the angels, namely Jesus, crowned with glory and honor because of the suffering of death, so that by the grace of God he might taste death for everyone. —Hebrews 2:9

Friar Maximilian Kolbe helped hide Jews from the Nazis during World War II until he was captured and imprisoned in the Auschwitz Concentration Camp. One day three men escaped the concentration camp, and in an effort to discourage other prisoners from attempting to escape, the Nazis ordered the execution of ten men. One of those randomly selected to be killed begged for mercy, and Kolbe selflessly stepped forward and offered to take the man's place.

Read Hebrews 2:9–10. God did not select an angel for the job of achieving our salvation. He selected His Son, Jesus Christ. Jesus was the only one suited for the task. He alone was perfectly positioned to taste death on behalf of humanity for the forgiveness of our sins. Our Messiah, our Savior, humbled Himself and became a man, so that He could become the author, the very source, of our salvation.

Jesus' suffering was not a way for Him to become *more* righteous or *more* moral. Rather, Jesus' suffering served to make Him our perfect Savior. That means Jesus is the Savior who can empathize with every hardship because He willingly endured it all as a man while also maintaining perfect obedience to the Father. Our Savior does not simply understand our suffering and temptations intellectually. He understands what it's like from firsthand experience. As a result, Jesus can perfectly relate to us and guide us through the sometimes painful, sometimes tempting, mires of life. Through His suffering, and by His salvation, we are no longer enemies. Nor are we simply His friends. By grace through faith, we become sons and daughters of the Father! Notice the text says "for a little while." Jesus' ministry and death on earth were not the end of His story. He returned to the right hand of the Father, and He's waiting to bring us to glory, the day that He returns and welcomes us into the eternal joy of God's presence.

Maximilian Kolbe willingly put himself between Jews and their Nazi oppressors. He was sent to one of the most horrific concentration camps, and while he was there he sacrificed himself in order to save another. What a beautiful reminder of our Savior's sacrifice. Our Lord humbled Himself and took our punishment upon Himself. In doing so, He made a way for each of us to be saved.

Reflection

Do you or someone you know have trouble accepting the forgiveness of God?

In what ways should Jesus' act of humbling Himself lower than the angels and becoming a man impact the way we serve others?

As you reflect on Christ's life, ministry, death, and Resurrection this Advent season, ask God's help in accepting the complete work of Christ's salvation and the fullness of God's forgiveness.

Day 34

Peace I leave with you; my peace I give to you. Not as the world gives do I give to you. Let not your hearts be troubled, neither let them be afraid. —John 14:27

In 2009, Bill Gates and fellow billionaire Warren Buffett founded the Giving Pledge, a campaign to encourage the world's billionaires to give away half of their wealth, either while they're living or upon their deaths. Bill Gates has said his children will only receive a small fraction of his wealth. The majority of his fortune will be given to philanthropic causes.

Read John 14:25–27. The promised Messiah had finally arrived, but in this passage, Jesus was preparing for His departure. He knew the redemption He was sent to secure on our behalf would lead to the Cross. However, He promised that the Holy Spirit would arrive to indwell believers after His death, Resurrection, and ascension. The Spirit teaches us, which is to say the Lord is living inside of us revealing to us things that were hidden and making known to us mysteries we formally did not understand. The Spirit is also inside of us, reminding us of all Jesus said and bringing to our attention Christ's words when we forget them (or perhaps when we simply choose to ignore them).

Christ wanted to make it clear that although He was leaving, He wasn't leaving us empty-handed. Not by a long shot. On the contrary, He left us with the very Spirit of God to live inside of us. He left us His peace, which is unlike anything in the world and is greater than any potion, concoction, or medication. His peace is the calm inside us when we experience difficulties, sickness, and loss. His peace comforts us when the news seems to only report wars, famines, and all kinds of disasters.

The Giving Pledge is an incredible display of charitable giving. In 2010, it was estimated the campaign had already raised $125 billion. As great as this act of generosity is, Christ left behind something more precious than money. He left His Spirit and His peace, neither of which can be bought.

Reflection

How would you describe the Holy Spirit to a friend?

In recent memory, in what ways has the Spirit taught you or comforted you? In what ways do you experience the movement of the Holy Spirit in your life?

Consider that the most valuable gift you can share this year may not be a physical object. Ask the Lord to show you ways to share your life and faith with the people you love.

Day 35

*May his name endure forever, his fame
continue as long as the sun! May people
be blessed in him, all nations call him
blessed!* —Psalm 72:17

*Y*ou have probably heard the term "one-
hit wonder." The expression refers to
celebrities, usually musicians, who
enjoy a brief flash of fame because of a single,
short-lived success. One example is the song
"Macarena" by Los Del Rio, which played nonstop for months and is still a party favorite.
The group, however, has not been heard from
again. There are countless examples of people
who enjoyed great fame at one time but have

since waned in popularity. Yuri Gargarin was the first man in space, but odds are the average person on the street wouldn't recognize the name. To say nothing of all the authors, actors, musicians, and politicians who at one time were the toast of the town but whose names have largely disappeared from popular vocabulary.

Read Psalm 72:17–19. The name of Jesus has continued to endure generation after generation, and His fame will continue to spread. Consider all the persecution in the history of the church and the violence and oppression aimed at God's children. Yet there has never been a successful campaign to wipe out God's people and suppress His glory and fame. In the two thousand years since His death and Resurrection, no one has ever dug up any dirt on Jesus or discredited His righteousness because there is no dirt to be found. There is no sin in our King. Our Lord, our righteous Savior, has drawn in billions of followers, and to this day His glory continues to spread into the biggest cities, the deepest jungle villages, and the remotest mountain tribes.

Fame is temporary and fleeting. For kings and pop stars and everyone in between, at some point, their fame peaks and then begins to decline. Not so with the Lord. His fame continues to grow and spread. Consider this: Jesus walked the earth two thousand years ago, and yet He is still the most famous man to ever live because He was and is more than just a man. His public ministry only lasted three years before He was crucified and buried in a borrowed tomb, and yet according to a 2010 Pew report, there are an estimated 2.2 billion professing Christians in the world. This is due to the fact that the ministry of the Lord didn't stop at His death because He rose again and lives on to this day. Jesus never sat down to write a bestselling book, and yet 100,000 Bibles are distributed every year and approximately 5 billion Bibles have been printed in total.

Reflection

In what ways have you witnessed the enduring fame of the Lord in your day-to-day life?

Are you actively contributing to the spread of Christ's glory? If so, how? If not, why?

Today's passage says we are blessed by Him. Take time to reflect on the ways you have recently experienced the blessings, joys, and satisfaction of His glory.

Day 36

*For he will save his people
from their sins.* —Matthew 1:21

If you had to guess, would you say that the
juice drink Snapple Apple has apple in its
ingredients? It might surprise you to learn
that the "apple" juice drink contains absolutely *no*
apples. Crazy, right? As it turns out, juice drinks
are not legally obligated to have ingredients that
match the name of the juice. That means you
could buy a drink called Strawberry Explosion,
and it doesn't have to contain any strawberry
whatsoever. Not all companies get off as easy
as Snapple, though. Not long ago, it was dis-
covered Volkswagen had rigged 11 million cars,

claiming they were environmentally friendly when in reality, the cars emitted an illegal level of carbon dioxide into the atmosphere. Unlike Snapple, this deception cost Volkswagen dearly when their stock dropped more than 50 percent.

Read Matthew 1:21c. Jesus did not come to help us hide our sins. He did not come to tell people that their sins were OK. He came to save His people; His mission is His name. Jesus' name literally means "Jehovah is salvation." This was what He came to do—to save His people from their sins. When Jesus came, a lot of people had a lot of different ideas about who He was and what He came to do. The same is true today. In reality, though, to understand Jesus, all we need to do is look at His name.

Jesus came to save people from every secret indiscretion and public moral failure, every self-ish thought and every lie. All throughout the Bible are stories of men and women who inter-ceded on behalf of others in order to save their lives. These kinds of selfless acts are present today, too, in the bravery of soldiers, the faith of martyrs, and the everyday selfless acts of people who make split-second decisions to step between others and certain disaster. However, there never has been and never will be a Savior who saves us from our sins other than Jesus Christ.

A lot of products out there claim to do some pretty incredible things. The truth is, many of them don't accomplish what they promise. And for those that deliver on their advertised uses, the question is, what kind of impact do they have on our lives in the long run? False advertisement is nothing new. Sometimes it's insignificant (like an apple juice that doesn't contain apples), and others times it makes national headlines (like when a major car company is caught in a lie). Thankfully, though, Jesus perfectly lived up to His name. He is salvation, and He has saved His people from their sins.

Reflection

Why do you think people have trouble accepting that Jesus will save them from their sins?

Have you ever been lied to or misled? How did that make you feel?

Thank God for never misleading you. Thank Jesus for being exactly who He says He is.

Day 37

For you will go out in joy and be led forth in peace; the mountains and the hills before you shall break forth into singing, and all the trees of the field shall clap their hands. —Isaiah 55:12

ahara Forest Project is a company that claims it can turn deserts into forests. Their plan: create solar power plants near oceans, desalinate saltwater (i.e., remove the salt) using power from the sun's heat, and use the distilled water to grow crops. Their ultimate goal is to turn desert sands into fertile farmland.

Read Isaiah 55:12–13. Isaiah 55 is an invitation from the Lord for people to forsake their unrighteousness and return to Him. How do we return? What is the path of our return? It is the way carved out by Christ. The route to God was unobstructed by Jesus through His death and Resurrection. And upon returning to the Lord through faith in Christ, we are to go out into the world with joy and peace and see the world with new eyes and a new heart. We will see all creation glorifying the Lord and celebrating Him with us.

The thornbush points back to the curse on the earth following the sin of Adam and Eve. Jesus came to break the curse of sin, to bring life where there was formerly death, to bring fruit where there was formerly barrenness. The nettle is a desert plant and, like the thorn bush, represents fruitlessness. However, the cypress and myrtle represent nobility, strength, life, and fruitfulness—in fact, the cypress tree was used by Solomon to construct the Temple and was highly prized.

The Lord's work in our lives stands as an enduring memorial to Him, a reminder of His accomplishments, and a testament for His glory and praise. Sahara Forest Project is transforming arid, lifeless desert into rich, vegetative farmland. Similarly, except on a much more incredible scale, our Lord has taken the spiritual lifelessness inside of us and transformed it into life and fruitfulness.

Reflection

Prior to God's work in your life, where was your spiritual lifelessness most evident?

After God's transformative work, in what ways has your new life become most evident?

Take time now to thank God for giving you new life through Christ and making your life fruitful. Pray that He will continue to reveal ways in which your life can become more fruitful for the glory of God and the good of others.

Day 38

I am the living bread that came down from heaven. —John 6:51

The 3D printer was invented in 1983, and since then, some strange things have been made using 3D-printing technology, such as guns, artificial limbs (for people and animals), recreations of old dinosaur bones, cars, and even houses. Perhaps the most unusual thing that has been 3D printed so far is food. That's right. Machines are now *printing* edible burgers and pizza.

Read John 6:46–51. Jesus was not saying we must literally eat something to have eternal life. There isn't some magic elixir or present-day manna from heaven we must physically ingest to be saved. Even if that were the case, even if God was still sending down manna from heaven, it wouldn't be enough to sustain us for long. As the Israelites who ate the miracle manna from heaven learned, it only sustained them for a day before they had to go out the next morning and collect more manna. Instead, Jesus referred to Himself when He talked about the bread of life. Rather, He alluded to His salvation achieved through His sacrifice. Jesus is our bread of life because He alone is the key to our eternal life. However, to enjoy the blessings of the bread of life, action is required on our part. We must eat. We must believe. We must have faith.

There are foods that claim to keep you awake, keep you full longer, and keep you looking young and beautiful. Even if these foods somehow make us feel stronger and younger, they will never compare with the bread of life. Yes, we have made incredible technological advances since the days of cooking wild game over an open campfire. We can 3D print food with machines now! As incredible as this is, though, technological leaps will never deliver the sustenance of the bread of life. Even the miracle manna from heaven only sustained the Israelites for a short while. Only the sustenance of the Lord, only the salvation of Jesus, will sustain us forever.

Reflection

What kinds of things does the world sell that people tend to put in the place of the Lord?

Why do you think it's often so difficult for people to accept that the things of the Lord are greater than the things of the world?

Thank God for sustaining you through the eternal redemption of Christ. Pray for those who are distracted by the things of the world that don't satisfy.

Day 39

But when the fullness of time had come,
God sent forth his Son, born of woman,
born under the law, to redeem those who
were under the law, so that we might
receive adoption as sons. —Galatians 4:4–5

*H*arriet Tubman was born a slave in Maryland in 1820 and escaped that slavery in 1849. Rather than remaining in hiding, looking out for herself and her own safety, Tubman returned to Maryland to help her family escape. However, she did not stop there. In the years that followed, Tubman made several trips into slave-holding states to help lead other slaves to freedom. It was dangerous work, of course, and at one point Tubman had a $40,000 bounty on her head. But the risk did not deter her. As a devout Christian, Tubman believed her work rescuing fellow slaves was accomplished with God's help. In all, Tubman made nineteen trips to slave-holding states and helped rescue more than three hundred slaves.

Read Galatians 4:1–7. Paul wrote that when the fullness of time had come, God sent Jesus. Jesus did not come when things looked OK or when the moment seemed good enough. God didn't randomly choose a time. There was a *right* time, a perfect moment, for the long-awaited Messiah to finally arrive. Jesus did not come a moment too soon or a moment too late. He came when the moment of His arrival had finally, fully come. This is when He delivered His redemption. In Greek, the word for *redeemed* means to pay a price for someone's freedom from the power of another, or to ransom, and this is exactly what our Savior did. At the right time, Jesus came to earth and paid the penalty for our sin, ransoming us from sin and death, and made a way for us to be received as children of God, sons and daughters of the Most High.

None of the slaves Harriet Tubman helped to rescue paid Tubman a penny for her services. They didn't promise to give Tubman anything in exchange for her help. Tubman believed it was her God-given duty to help her fellow slaves. Even more so, Christ made a way for us to be saved without requiring any works in return. Jesus made a way for us to receive adoption into the family of God. We do not earn the status of child of God. We receive it through God's grace and Christ's sacrifice. It is through Christ alone, apart from any work or effort of our own, that we can call God our Abba, Father.

Reflection

Why do you think some people prefer to think of God as distant and detached, rather than close like a Father?

Are you sometimes tempted to try to earn God's affection and loyalty? Why do you suppose that is?

Ask God to show you how you can take the message of Christ's redemption and bring it to those in slavery to sin, helping to free as many as you can.

Day 40

You know that he appeared in order to take away sins, and in him there is no sin.
—1 John 3:5

In many countries around the globe, presidents have the ability to pardon criminals. This is true in the United States, where the president has the power to shorten someone's prison sentence or pardon a convict completely. George Washington issued sixteen pardons during his presidency, and other presidents have followed suit. In fact, President Franklin D. Roosevelt issued a staggering 3,687 pardons. A presidential pardon essentially wipes a person's slate clean and renews a person's status of innocence.

Read 1 John 3:1–5. Everyone is a child of God in the sense that each of us was made by Him and in His image. In these verses, John referred to an exclusive, unique sense in which believers are considered children of God. Through faith, we are those adopted into God's family and made coheirs with Christ in the kingdom of God.

There are many misconceptions nowadays about who Jesus was and what He stood for. Some people believe Jesus was a good guy who simply wanted people to live moral lives. Consequently, there is also a misconception that Jesus simply wanted His followers to be good men and women who live moral lives. As we know, though, Jesus was and is so much more than a "good guy." He is Lord, King, and Savior. Jesus did not come to earth to make us more likable, more successful, or better behaved. As we read in verse 5, Jesus came to take away our sins and make us righteous, just as He is righteous.

A president might choose to pardon someone for a variety of reasons . . . maybe the person was charged with a crime unfairly, or perhaps they have proven themselves to be rehabilitated. Whatever the case, the president has the authority to free people from prison and wipe their legal slate clean. Jesus, though, has the power to pardon people in ways the president can't. Through His sacrifice, Jesus made a way for each of us to be pardoned. This pardon is not offered to us because we've been well behaved. Rather, the pardon Jesus purchased for us by His blood is given to us as a free gift. His pardon takes away our sin—He frees us from the control of sin and takes away the penalty of our sin—and brings us into the family of God.

Reflection

When you think about Christ's pardon, what emotions does it evoke (gratitude, humility, joy)?

In what ways does your life reflect Christ's pardon—His salvation—to the world around you?

Thank Jesus for His salvation, the gift of His unmerited pardon, and ask the Lord to create greater gratitude in your heart this Advent season. Pray that your joy for His salvation and your hope for His return will spill over into the lives of others.

**If you enjoyed this book,
will you consider sharing the message with others?**

Let us know your thoughts at
info@newhopepublishers.com. You can also let the author know
by visiting or sharing a photo of the cover on our social media pages or
leaving a review at a retailer's site. All of it helps us get the message out!

Twitter.com/NewHopeBooks

Facebook.com/NewHopePublishers

Instagram.com/NewHopePublishers

———————

New Hope® Publishers, Ascender Books, Iron Stream Books,
and New Hope Kidz
are imprints of Iron Stream Media,
which derives its name from Proverbs 27:17,
"As iron sharpens iron, so one person sharpens another."

This sharpening describes the process of discipleship, one to another.
With this in mind, Iron Stream Media provides a variety of solutions for
churches, ministry leaders, and nonprofits ranging from in-depth Bible
study curriculum and Christian book publishing to custom publishing
and consultative services. Through the popular Life Bible Study and
Student Life Bible Study brands, ISM provides web-based full-year and
short-term Bible study teaching plans as well as printed devotionals,
Bibles, and discipleship curriculum.

For more information on ISM and its imprints, please visit

IronStreamMedia.com

NewHopePublishers.com

CHRISTMAS FICTION FROM
NEW HOPE PUBLISHERS

VISIT **NEWHOPEPUBLISHERS.COM**
FOR MORE INFORMATION.

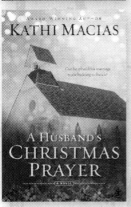